THERE, I SAID IT

BOB DYLAN IS OVERRATED

and a few other carefully considered objections

to the greatest musicians of all time

by various authors

edited by Joshua Shelov

THERE, I SAID IT: BOB DYLAN IS OVERRATED

and a few other carefully considered objections

to the greatest musicians of all time

Copyright © 2016 Joshua Shelov

For Jennifer, Owen, Emma, and Andrew

TABLE OF CONTENTS

INTRODUCTION

This is not a hate book. Lord knows there's enough hate float-ing around out there, souring up the internet, sludging up CNN.

This book is a confession. Or, a series of confessions, as it were. My fellow writers and I come from all walks of life. But we all write from a place of hope, fueled not by a desire to diminish oth-ers, but by a yearning to connect *with* others.

With this book, we are reaching out in what feels like a pummeling darkness of other people's certainty, seeking someone out there, anyone, who shares our secret confusion. Our subjects are many. But our message is the same. And that message is this:

Bob Dylan is terrible, and if you like him, you are also terri-ble.

OK. What happened there is that a little hate leaked out by accident. I told a little joke. OK? That's all. I apologize.

This tends to happen to me when I get going about Bob Dy-lan, or worse yet, his acolytes, somewhere in Brooklyn, no doubt, chests puffed out beneath their beards, breath befouled by the microbrew *du jour,* bloviating without a hint of equivocation about Dylan's unquestioned spot on music's Mount Rushmore, alongside Coltrane, Elvis, and The Beatles.

I have only one objection to this notion. And that is this:

The Beatles sang like God's own children and their music united the world. Whereas Bob Dylan – stay with me here, because this is scientifically provable – sings like Daniel Day-Lewis in *My Left Foot* being pulled violently from his wheelchair and drowned in a sink.

See, there I go again.

Let me try once more. Let me breathe deep, and attempt to capture the true, deeper, benevolent spirit of this book. This book was born on Facebook, after all, a much smiley-facier corner of the interwebs than Twitter. On March 18th, 2014, I posted "Who is the greatest, most legendary artist that you just don't get? The most acclaimed, profound genius who just leaves you cold? Mine's Bob Dylan. Who's yours?"

Kaboom. Within a few hours, 275 friends had contributed their own blasphemous confessions. Here were Beatle-phobes, Zep-sinkers, and Stones-throwers. Turns out, anyone who is anyone in the field of music has someone out there – whole tribes of someones – who cannot for the life of them figure out what the fuss is all about.

And that's really what this book is about. It's not about Bob Dylan, and how his voice can sadden the dead. No. It's about you finding your secret tribe.

Did you even know you had a secret tribe? Well, guess what. You do. Your secret tribe is the group of people who just skimmed through the same table of contents you just skimmed through, and said, "YES. I ALWAYS KNEW Tom Waits wasn't actually a recording artist, but in fact an elaborate practical joke."

Guess what. You're right. The proof is right here. It says so, right here in these pages. The emperor is, in fact, buck naked.

So: who's your blind spot? Who's the star who hangs in your sky, but stubbornly refuses to shine? Who's that singer who can't POSSIBLY be a legend, but who somehow, impossibly, is?

See? This isn't hate. This is community.

You're not alone.

Unless you like Bob Dylan.

In which case you are much, much worse than alone.

You're deaf.

TOM WAITS

by Amy Wilson

When I was a freshman in college, the coolest thing about me was nothing. I could see that before I even unpacked; I just wasn't sure where to begin. I was so uncool that I didn't even know what it was about me that was the uncoolest. (It was my hair. Then again, it was the late '80s.)

I figured that the quickest route to any sense of co-ed belonging - and eventual coolness - was participation in everything college life had to offer. So that fall I pulled a Marcia Brady and signed up for everything on campus, from fencing to the gospel choir. And due to powers that remain beyond my understanding, I got into an improv comedy group, which seemed very cool indeed. It meant instant membership in a clique of stimulating and hilarious friends.

The problem is that every moment with a make-something-funny-up-right-now group of people is rather stressful; there is this constant need to be - well, funny. Or at least informative. Or at least certain about the choice you are making by choosing to speak words aloud. Freshman year, I mostly spoke when spoken to. I was a little bit afraid of our director, who wore combat boots and had hung out at CBGB a few times (whatever that was) while he was still in high school. Jeff was very funny. He was also the hardest to make laugh. But he knew cool, and it seemed clear that if I just shadowed him and the other upperclassmen in the group - and liked what they liked - there would be hope for me yet.

By spring break, I almost felt like I belonged. My comedy group was going on a spring break tour, to dazzle boarding school audiences from New Haven to Charleston and back again. The dozen or so of us piled into three cars and set off on I-95 South on a mid-March afternoon. I was in the middle of the back seat in what felt to me like the coolest car. Jeff, as our director, was taking the first turn at the wheel.

My college years coincided with the dawn of CDs, but they were still sort of fringe. These were the days of cassettes: of listening to a single album all the way through, over and over again, the songs in the order the artist intended, until the tape actually warped from overuse. (I had been obliged to buy several copies of Steve Miller Band's *Abracadabra*, back when I had been even less cool.) It was also the days of whoever was driving getting to decide whose album you were going to listen to, which still seems to me like it was only fair.

"Tom Waits," Jeff announced at our first red light, holding his homemade cassette case (with Bic-pen artwork) aloft. My fellow passengers oohed and aahed at what was clearly an absolutely perfect choice. I said nothing.

"Do *you* like Tom Waits?" Jeff said, turning around and looking right at me. Perhaps my lack of immediate assent had irked him.

"I-- don't know," I admitted. "I don't think I've ever heard him."

Everyone in the car gasped in disbelief.

"He's amazing," Jeff said with great authority, and everyone else in the car nodded, rolling their eyes at how unnecessary that should have been for him even to say.

The guy riding shotgun popped in the cassette. I waited eagerly for my life to be changed, to know who Tom Waits was and to be cool at last.

Then Cookie Monster started singing.

Or was it Rolf? It was definitely a Muppet.

I waited for Jeff to burst out laughing, pop out the cassette, but his eyes were on the road. My seatmates in the back closed their eyes and listened, nodding their heads as if at church.

I wondered if everyone in the car was playing a trick on me.

Then I figured maybe Tom Waits was really high-concept. Maybe this was a character he was working for this particular song? Maybe this was a *Spoon River Anthology* sort of album, and for the next song he'd sing as a carnival busker, a crooning traveling salesman.

But then the next song started, and he sounded exactly the same.

Jeff looked up at me in the rear view mirror, truly savoring this moment. He had introduced me to a master.

"What do you think?" he asked.

"Does he-- *have* to sing like that?" I asked back.

Three heads swiveled to face me in unified confusion. (Jeff, thank goodness, barely managed to continue to drive.)

"I mean, does he have a regular voice?" I stammered. "And if he does, why doesn't he just use that one?"

Jeff looked at me in the rear-view mirror, then back at the road. I could see his disappointment in me from the way he set his jaw.

"Tom Waits is amazing," he said, quite sure of himself.

We listened to the rest of *Rain Dogs* in silence.

For a quarter of a century, for all of my adult life, I have carried with me the certainty that Tom Waits' gravelly bark is a sort of dog-whistle for cool, that the people who like Tom Waits, people like Jeff, literally hear something in his voice that I cannot, that I never will, because I lack some crucial bit of DNA. My spirit is willing, but my ears are weak.

But riding in that back seat that day was at least a lesson in self-acceptance. I could see clearly, even at that moment, that I'd never be cool enough to like Tom Waits. And I was cool with that.

ERIC CLAPTON

by Alex Funk

Is Clapton actually God?

Having grown up Unitarian, I'm inclined to demand a relatively high burden of proof. So let's begin with this: whatever claim Sir Eric has to godhead status finds no basis in his singing or songwriting. The former quality achieves invisibility on good days, tediousness on bad ones. The latter trait might initially appear more laudable. But consider some of the EC-associated hits that he had no hand whatsoever in writing:

> "For Your Love" (1965)
>
> "Crossroads" (1966)
>
> "While My Guitar Gently Weeps" (1968)
>
> "White Room" (1968)
>
> "After Midnight" (1970)
>
> "I Shot the Sheriff "(1974)
>
> "Cocaine" (1977)

Here are three more pillars upon which the Clapton legend is built:

"Sunshine of Your Love" (1967)

"Layla" (1971)

"Tears in Heaven" (1992)

Slowhand gets co-writer credit on these, and in each case we know what he contributed. He wrote the bridge to "Sunshine" ("I've been waiting so long..."). That is indeed a snappy little bridge, and hats off for it.

Now: think of your favorite half of "Layla": is it the first three minutes of chugging, bluesy "Got me on my knees," or the strangely powerful coda, with rootsy piano and twanging guitars almost tangibly stretching out for the unattainable? Yeah, that second part was written by Jim Gordon, and that distinctive high guitar line was played by Duane Allman.

But wait! You cry. Clapton wrote a couple of (semi-) legendary songs all by himself:

"Wonderful Tonight"

"My Father's Eyes"

I simply cannot stand the first, and know several women who think that, *pace* Patti Boyd, any person non-ironically writing that song in their honor would accomplish nothing more or less than serious nightmare fulfillment. The second is a cynical, gospel-

cloaked return to the personal anguish well that flowed so lucra-
tively with "Heaven." These are not great songs, and arguably not
even good.

So, then, to the heart of the matter: to love Eric Clapton is to
love his guitar playing. (Duh.) Proselytizers attempt to sell me on
two aspects of that axework: dexterity and tone. With the first I can
be impressed but never obsessed: the conflation of hours logged or
riffs mastered with actual artistic accomplishment is one of the
quintessential Fallacies of Youth. Does Clapton rise above Steve Vai
in this regard, or Jeff Beck, or Joe Satriani? If it's a tie, we need fur-
ther justification for Eric's outsized reputation.

Then tone, the last redoubt of musical subjectivity. Let me
attempt to situate Clapton's tone within the context of some legendary neighbors at the blues-rock interface: Jimi Hendrix, B.B.
King, and Jimmy Page. Though each created his own unique pal-
ette, the three neighbors have in common guitar playing that is at
times 'blistering,' 'huge,' 'raw.' King's punches you in the chest,
even in studio recordings; Hendrix's soars, sets things on fire; Page's
goes in and out of tune, of white noise, of intelligibility.

Clapton's tone, on the other hand, is restrained. Thoughtful.
Brooding. "Flawless and impeccable," adds a Clapton-loving
friend. These are all positive things. But who ever went to a rock or
blues concert for impeccable thoughtfulness?

Tonally speaking, I find Clapton much closer to Mark Knopfler, another six-string virtuoso with a thoughtful side and a perfectionist streak. And it's personal, sure, but I find Knopfler's playing warmer, more open, less studied and self-conscious.

Here are five songs Knopfler wrote by himself during the eight years in which Dire Straits was an active band:

"Sultans of Swing" (1978)
"Romeo and Juliet" (1981)
"Telegraph Road" (1982)
"Walk of Life" (1985)
"Brothers in Arms" (1985)

I'll take these five over the Clapton credits above, which are culled from a greater-than-30-year span. Knopfler and Dire Straits are still waiting to hear from the Rock and Roll Hall of Fame, which in the meantime has seen fit to induct Eric Clapton not once, not twice, but three separate times.

Surely I can't be alone in listening to Clapton like a Unitarian at a Catholic mass, eager to genuflect out of peer pressure and re-spect, but tormented by the hypocrisy of accepting the tripartite glory of a deity he struggles to believe in at all. The hand slips awkwardly back toward the thigh, Derek demoted (Dominoes in tow) from iPod to backup drive.

CAROLE KING

by Danielle Delgado

I was a small child when Carole King's 'landmark' *Tapestry* album was released. I remember humming along with the songs that were everywhere: "...You make me feel like a natural woman ..." " ... I'll be there ... you've got a friend ..." "...It's too late, baby ..." They were friendly and welcoming tunes; even the ones intended to be Sad ("But will you love me tomorrow?...") were insistently catchy. I was a child, and I hummed along with the warbling, vigorously upbeat lady.

I've since searched deep within myself each time I've heard or read the adulation that now so regularly seems to come Carole King's way – in critical essays, blogs, passing mentions in articles about influential music of note, over lunch with peers ("Oooh, I love this song! She's so great!"), and lately with the opening of a new biographical Broadway musical showcasing her 'soundtrack to a generation.'

Because now, as an adult, no less an adult woman, the songs of Carole King make me cringe, mostly. And when I say as much, my statement is met with derision and the swift revoking of my Woman Card.

I'm rather unsure why. Her songwriting reputation was established co-penning a tsunami of certified pop hits and now-standards...*with her husband.* The only thing I can figure is that the apex of her stardom as a solo artist coincided with the second-wave feminism of the 70's, thereby cementing her place on the Mount Rushmore of Female Empowerment.

Her iconic status certainly can't be due to her actual music, can it? Her solo output was certainly hummable – but so are nursery rhymes. I hear metabolism-freezing, reductive fructose in her lyrics, juvenile and/or undiagnosed co-dependency in her content, and reed-thin quality of voice (there's a reason you hear covers of her songs (Aretha, James Taylor; etc.) more often than her own versions, methinks).

I get that these things make her *relatable* - there's certainly no shortage of jejune, neurotic women of average voice out there - but I guess I just don't want to believe that relatability alone makes her an artist that aliens would be informed is representative of my gender's power of expression.

There is only one Carole King song I can say I like, despite the girlish silliness of its words: "I feel the earth move under my feet / I feel the sky tumbling down / I feel my heart start to trembling / Whenever you're around..."

It brings a smile to my face as I hear someone with little innate funk determined to be funky, like The Little Train That Could. Like the rest of us who love music but can't make music ourselves. I've heard modern art equated as "I Could Do That + Yeah, But You Didn't." Maybe that's the core of my aversion.

Carole King made the most of making stuff up that I possibly could have when I was 6, but didn't. And somehow she's revered for it, while I am a traitor to my kind. This is not her fault, of course – she seems like a nice enough lady (to whom I can apparently only refer by full name, like a brand(™). Just don't put me on hold or in an elevator with her tunes, please. I might be tempted to hum along. And become aware of how far I haven't come.

THE WHO

By Aimee Weingart Pollak

Every couple of years I meet someone, usually a woman around my age, and take an instant dislike to her. On the surface, we should be friends. Our kids are on the same soccer team, we grew up in the same town, we both like yoga, we both hate bananas. We even have some friends in common. Yet, despite outward signs pointing toward compatibility, I just can't stand her.

That's sort of how I feel about The Who.

I'm friends with most of The Who's friends. I hit it off immediately with Pink Floyd and Led Zeppelin - we were BFF's all through high school. I had a two-year love affair with Eric Clapton, culminating in a slow dance at prom. I gave in to a drunken one-night stand with The Clash in 11th grade. And Queen has been my gay best friend since we met on the first day of chorus.

But The Who and I could never get past grudging acquaintances: that forced head nod as you pass each other in the hall. *Sup.*

After high school, The Who and I went our separate ways, thank God. I hooked up with classic jazz in an East Village record shop, and never looked back. Hard bop and I were soon inseparable. We drank ourselves blind on shitty red wine, Coltrane and Miles and me. I fell in love on a cliche New York City fire escape, flying on *Kind of Blue.*

And then, in the blink of an eye, I was married and suburban, belly swollen in a starter home. Soon my music collection was as bloated and misshapen as I was. My five-CD changer spun a hideous Lazy Susan of Laurie Berkner, Raffi and the Wiggles.

Running into The Who again was the furthest thing from my mind.

And then. One day.

I was neck-deep in my minivan, kids asleep in the back. I sneaked a hit of low-volume Eminem. I remember driving the long way home, through my old neighborhood. Fate even found me a parking spot. Pushing a groggy double stroller down those memory-soaked streets, I felt the unmistakable tug of nostalgia for my fumbling classic rock days. It felt like only yesterday that Pink Floyd was nibbling at my ears, while I lay in the back seat of that '81 Monte Carlo, my shirt pushed up to my armpits by the overeager boy.

But this was now, and someone had put on a ring on it. After months of skulking around the edges of the playground, I was thrilled to have scored a hot invite to a cool-mom wine-and-lunch playdate. I spent the morning worrying that my not-quite-toilet-trained kid would pee on the cool mom's sofa. It never occurred to me that *I* would be the problem.

I was on my third-and-a-halfth glass of pinot grigio when *Pinball Wizard* hit the Bose. In a flash, I was a teenager again. I looked around at my fellow moms, instinctively rolling my eyes, making a "gagging" face. The moms stared back at me in shock. I realized - way too late - that they were reacting with pleasure, even joy, at The Who's arrival.

I retreated into myself for a second, listening to the music for clues. Some deaf kid was being led into a game room by a pack of disciples. I tried my damndest to appreciate the sounds pummeling my eardrums. Nope. The Who was still that same old schmuck from high school, now trying to hide behind a combover and a salesman's plastic smile. Same as the old boss.

But *Jesus,* look at these new friends of mine, cooing along when the guitars drop out: *sure, plays, a-mean, pin, ball.* Like he's still the coolest guy, *evar.*

Now I run into this fucking asshole everywhere I go. The Who is all over their book clubs and mah jongg groups, even their kids' birthday parties. Their husbands invite him to Friday night poker and Sunday morning tailgates. When he shows up at our favorite bar, I grit out a smile and walk into the next room, avoiding ear contact. As often as not, I'm forced to give The Who an insincere hello, telling him how good he looks (is that a new shirt? did you lose weight?) and pretending to be interested in his latest tour (how the *hell* are they still touring??). Even our ski vacations provide me with no escape. Lifties *love* The Who. At the least my helmet dulls the pain.

The absolute nadir was 2010, when The Who played halftime of the Super Bowl. Our entire g-g-generation screamed along to "Who Are You." I was disgusted. Then my husband joined in. I turned to him with icy eyes. This was the final straw.

On the car ride home, I laid down the law. There could be no casual friendship with The Who. I would not be fooled again. He couldn't agree with me in private about The Who being the worst, and then jump right in with The Who and his buddies for a cigar out on the patio. Maybe I was being unreasonable. Fine. But he was going to have to take one for the team.

I remember his hand hovering over the radio station presets. I waited anxiously for his choice. He picked AltNation. My new best friend Muse sang to me about resistance. And I fell in love with my husband all over again. I was back on the fire escape. Free.

In the end, he said it was an easy decision for him. After all, The Who would never open its heart or legs to him. See me, feel me, touch me, bitches.

U2

by Jason Barker

For children of the '70s, the first experience of U2 was probably a grainy video, seen during the MTV-when-it-played-music era: guys in black leather, singing on a barge in an industrial-looking port. The song, probably "New Year's Day," was good. A hit. So, OK: here's a new band that plays real instruments and writes catchy, substantial songs. Great.

Cut to a few years later, and my middle school friends talking about how great U2 is, with their "heavy" lyrics. OK. "I Still Haven't Found What I'm Looking For" is fine. The guitar bit with heavy delay thing is pretty cool.

Over the decades to come, though, we hear as much about Bono at Davos, meeting Desmond Tutu and heads of state, and cutting live to Sarajevo under siege during a stadium show as we do about music. A headline in *The Financial Times* recently read, "U2 singer Bono joins Bank of America in pursuit of common goals."

Most of us, unless we are involved directly in policy, charity, or public service, experience moments when we feel our work is inadequate to the world's challenges or injustices. That feeling could be more acute for those involved in entertainment. U2 (mostly in the form of Bono) has responded by vigorously throwing itself into the public arena as advocates for a variety of good causes. However, at some point, a rock band is a bunch of guys (now aging a bit) paid money to play music and shake their asses around on stage. Nothing will ever change that.

So here's my question: how good does a band have to be to smooth the transition from pop music to the truly-weighty? Is the platonic ideal of the rock and roll band capable of delivering a listener from her seat in an arena to a distant nation experiencing famine? Do the main songwriters from this ideal rock band take a break from the whole pop music thing and make *Spider Man: Turn off the Dark?*

I remember the moment well that I became entirely unable to see U2 as anything other than a stadium-filling rock act (no shame in that, by the way). It was a highlight from the Zooropa tour (I think) when Bono took a break from the songs to lunge out at the crowd and announce to the audience that he had a live feed to Sarajevo, where people dodging mortars and sniper fire would share their experiences.

I'm sorry, but I'll take The Clash giving the finger to the Queen any day. It's only rock and roll, but, you know.

THE BEATLES

By Brian Alverson

As a pediatric hospitalist, I care for children with a wide variety of genetic problems. Every once in a while, I encounter a disability that is astonishingly specific. For example, a child with *trimethylaminuria* can't smell rotten fish. Another child, diagnosed with *hereditary sensory neuropathy type I,* can't feel heat. Another with *achromatopsia* can't see colors. And so on into minutia.

Most health professionals will begrudgingly admit that we are prone to overdiagnosing ourselves with the diseases we treat. This tendency likely stems from the basic human desire to wrestle understanding out of the inexplicable twinges and tingles of inexorable human aging, paired with an unusually broad knowledge base of potential causes, however far-flung.

So, with this caveat in mind – and admitting full well that I might very well be falling into the physician's classic psychological trap – I have diagnosed myself with a most unusual genetic syndrome: *beatlagnosia.* This is, of course, the rare genetic inability to appreciate The Beatles.

I have loved and appreciated a broader range of music than most. I am in my 40s, and therefore still like to have my hands physically palpating the disc as I select it, as opposed to downloading it down from some electronic cloud floating somewhere above the Indian subcontinent.

As a violinist, I have enjoyed and played all manner of classical works, from Bach to Schoenberg. But I am no classical snoot. A perusal through my CD collection will reveal works from Ray Charles and James Brown to AC/DC and Dolly Parton. I've got favorite songs that nobody's heard of, like Jimmy Sturr's "Fiddlemania Polka" (the first dance at my wedding), as well as just about any song by the remarkable Russian-folk-rockabilly band, Limpopo.

But the Beatles? Well, they've just escaped me. When this foppish boy band descended on America (admittedly, six years before my birth), and the hordes of screaming bob-haired girls streamed onto the tarmac to devour them, an entire generation was defined. Countless boy bands have followed, but none has met with anywhere near the success of the Fab Four. The Beatles are lauded, routinely, as the greatest rock band who ever lived.

Objectively, I must concur. As Stephen Colbert might say, "the market has spoken." I cannot deny that how we define great art is and should be affected by our acceptance that if a huge percentage of the population decides something is great, it must therefore be. The market has spoken, and the Beatles are, without a doubt, the greatest band of all time.

But I couldn't care less. I'm a true believer in common humanity as a measure of artistic value. I can appreciate Lady Gaga. Wearing a meat-dress was a stroke of genius. And her competition with Miley Cyrus re: who can make parents cringe the hardest must be viewed on some level as a solid artistic outing.

But my *beatlagnosia* is incurable. The Beatles remain a blind spot in my field of vision. I cannot accept their music as anything but a series of notes and beats.

Stranger still, my inability to enjoy The Beatles seems to be limited to the group, not the individuals. I'll confess to tapping my toe to George Harrison's "I've Got My Mind Set On You." I've teared up a bit at "Imagine," inevitably played to lit candles, accompanying some far-off human atrocity. (I hasten to add that my slight weakness for Beatles-as-solo-artists doesn't extend to Ringo. I may be sick, but I'm not stupid.)

Did my children inherit my condition? I suppose time will tell. Right now, they're too busy banging cups around the kitchen and sing-screaming to Katy Perry.

But someday, when they're grumpy adolescents, fingering through dad's old CD collection, maybe they'll find my copy of the White Album, still wrapped in its plastic. Perhaps they'll unwrap it, and the first strains of "Back in the U.S.S.R." will find their way out of the speakers.

When that moment comes, I'll be on the lookout for that blank stare of incomprehension. That's when I'll know if they've caught the family disease.

BILLY JOEL

by David Bauer

I'm a massage fan. Whether your stress is of the physical or emotional variety, when your body starts cramping and betraying you, there's nothing more satisfying than putting it in the hands of a confident professional.

There are risks involved, of course. Total muscular relaxation during the course of an intense full-body massage is impossible, if you get my drift. I can't speak for all men, but I think a lot of guys out there will agree that, beyond the good feeling, a 60-minute massage really boils down to two things: an hour spent trying not to fart, and praying you don't get an erection. While the former is all dieting and genetics (and as an overweight Jew of Eastern European descent, I'm pretty much fucked on both counts), I have a foolproof method of avoiding the latter. As soon as that masseuse lays her hands on me...the instant she starts kneading those knots out of my shoulders, and my eyes start to close...all I have to do is start reciting Billy Joel lyrics in my head. For nothing in this great, God-fearing world makes me more flaccid than a Billy Joel tune.

Bottle of red....bottle of WHITE...it all depends on your appetite....

When I'm lying there, nude but for a towel (yes: I go all the way), with nature sounds trickling away in the background, and the scent of incense teasing me...as soon as she starts greasing those hands up, and nature begins its fateful pull...all I have to do is hitch a ride with Brenda and Eddie and Mr. Cacciatore down the streets of Allentown or Hackensack or wherever this fucking Long Island Lunatic is taking me in his absolutely psychotic scenarios. I mean, what the HELL is this guy talking about?? Thankfully, my penis doesn't stand a chance.

Then suddenly, she ups the ante. Without warning, she's putting those skilled, tantalizing fingers on my chest, rubbing in concentric circles. My thoughts drift away. My vice-like grip on the melody loosens. Rookie mistake. Never attempt powering through without the Joel. I'm almost at half-mast before I realize it. I need to dig deep. *You need - to learn - to pace yourself....PRESSURE! You're just like everybody else...PRESSURE!!!!*

Soft. Phew, that was a close one.

It should be smooth sailing from here on out. But it never is. She starts working my neck. I call up an old reliable: the whistling-man intro from *The Stranger.* I got this. I start to relax and enjoy...but I take a wrong turn, and it morphs into the opening to *The Winds of Change* by the Scorpions. I'm immediately rock-hard. Quick, before she notices! *Uptown Girl...she's been living in her white-*

35

bread world. Praise the lord! A millionaire multi-platinum recording artist's song about being on the wrong end of a class struggle shrivels me up but good.

But now I'm rattled. Why do I even get massages?!?!?! This is no way to live! And with my defenses down, she's moves up to my head. My Achilles heel. My Achilles head. I need to go all out before its too late. I need Bad Sound Effects Billy Joel. The nadir, 80's Bar Mitzvah dance era. *And we were SHARP.*
As sharp as KNIVESKNIVESKNIVESKNIVES.

It's not working! I pull the emergency brake: *TELLLLLLL HERRR ABOUT IT....AND* soft.

The rest is a blur. Some smooth douchiness from *An Innocent Man* gets me through the feet. *The Ballad of Billy the Kid* keeps it nice and copacetic during the thighs. I didn't even need to use my ace in the hole, *River of Dreams.* Eh, you can never be too careful. *In the middle of the naigh-ai-aight...*

Umm...is she getting a little too close to my johnson? Oh no oh no oh no. *Captain Jack will getcha high tonight! And take you to your special island!* We got it Billy, you're singing about drugs. Goddamn it, this isn't working! I'm going 100% full outright now. All the questionable arrangements, bizarre tempo changes. THE

WEIRD HIGH VOICES IN THE CHORUS OF WE DIDN'T START THE FIRE! C'mon!

Oh wait...this is one of THOSE massage parlors? Heh, this is kinda embarrassing. *I follow the Moskva....down to Gorky Park...listening to the Wind of Cha-ange....*

JOHN COLTRANE

by James Michels

I will start with what I will not say. I do not categorically hate jazz music. I have displayed Miles Davis and Chicago proudly in my collection for a number of years. Much of the music I do enjoy owes a great debt of gratitude to Duke Ellington arrangements, to the vocal stylings of a Ray Charles, the songwriting abilities of a Billy Strayhorn. I like jazz. And much of it I love.

I understand, of course, why John Coltrane is part of the modern music pantheon. He was a giant who carefully controlled and arranged his output, to maximum effect, with minimum waste.

Yet when I play *Giant Steps,* no track speaks to me. All I hear is a cacophony of horns, a smashing of drums. A string bass painfully out of place. Pianos that I find neither uplifting nor groundbreaking. No track there meets my five-second rule.

Mind you, I find my own lack of understanding acutely painful. Jazz artists I do 'get,' such as Wynton Marsalis, insist that they never would have started had Coltrane not shown the way.

I do retain an odd side effect. Not enjoying Coltrane's widely-acclaimed masterpieces has led me to curate the works I do enjoy that much more. I do not collect, or take for granted, works "alleged" to be great. I require music to pass my own smell test.

For that reason, John Coltrane remains that conspicuous space in my record collection. He is the one I was clearly meant to enjoy someday...yet that day never came.

THE SMITHS

by Andrew McLaughlin

After I broke up with my girlfriend Rinne back in 1998, I found myself in a barren sublet in the East Village, jobless, alone. The apartment had a bunch of CDs; so I would lie on the floor and put on music to match my misery.

Bonnie Raitt: perfect.

Richard and Linda Thompson: Of course.

And then: The Smiths. Obviously, I thought, the Smiths are just what I need.

But: Nothing. Their songs were hollow, empty, trite.

Catchy, sometimes, but never moving.

It felt like a parody of sad teen music, more than actual depth.

And in that way, helped me get over myself.

THE ROLLING STONES

by Cebra Graves

I blame my parents for my frigidity in the face of The Rolling Stones.

That's the best deflection before starting in on self-flagellation, right? As I make my long private shame public, I can at least indict them along with myself, no? They were closer to the action and therefore more culpable.

That's the theory I came up with after a session with my music therapist Chris Molanphy, when forced to introspect on why I do not 'feel' the...excitement? Genius? Artistry?...of "The World's Greatest Rock and Roll Band." Like any good therapist, he listened attentively and offered support. He said he'd long had a fascination with my condition, and the first question on the standard diagnostic instrument was whether my lack of appreciation stemmed from being on 'Team Beatles.' He prescribed listening to Soundcheck's Beatles vs. Stones "Smackdown Sessions" (google it) to get more closely in touch with my feelings.

This proved helpful. The Beatles tunes lit up my cortex, while the Stones songs flatlined. I knew most of them, but realized I'd had only the slightest exposure to them in my youth. It wasn't so much that I was on 'Team Beatles' as that I've never even realized there was a major rivalry.

My parents existed only on the periphery of the Stones/Beatles fight. Born in 1940, three years before Mick and Keith, my father's rebel music was bebop, blues and early rock: Charlie Parker, Lester Young, Mingus and Miles, Ray Charles, BB King, Bo Diddley and Chuck Berry. My mother was the right age, but too far afield: a folkie, whose vinyl was heavy on The Kingston Trio and Pete Seeger, Joan Baez and Peter, Paul and Mary.

If popular culture is viral, then my home was the perfect petri dish for growing a Stones vaccine. As a boy, I might have heard "Brown Sugar" or "Jumpin' Jack Flash" on the radio, but I was dancing to "Johnny B. Goode" and singing along to "This Land Is Your Land."

But, but! - I asked my therapist - I thought that pop virality operated via peers, not parents. He had a ready answer: The Stones were (relatively) shitty in the 1980s. My early inoculation proved easily resistant to "Undercover" and "Dirty Work"; and by the time "Steel Wheels" came around, I was so far removed from mainstream rock (immersed in the likes of R.E.M., The Pogues and They Might Be Giants) that infection was unlikely at best.

Unfortunately, despite the intellectual, er, satisfaction of this explanation, my shame persists. Because even today, The Rolling Stones are the *ne plus ultra* of attitude, the epitome of badass sexiness, the legends of swagger. Logically, then, by not feeling them (is there a Yiddishism for 'in my crotch'?) I am uncool. Neutered. A salaryman. A nerd. I tell myself that there are enough objectively 'true rock' acts that I am able to connect with—The Ramones, Bruce Springsteen, Nirvana—that I can't be a total eunuch.

And yet. And yet.

[Camera fades on a solitary figured shadowed on a couch, head in hands. "Paint It Black" swells in the background.]

FRANK SINATRA

by Nancy Anderson

I confess I don't understand why Frank Sinatra is considered the finest interpreter of the Great American Songbook in history. First, my credentials: I make my living interpreting that same songbook. But I assure you, this is not a matter of sour grapes. I've felt this way ever since I can remember.

My father was a pianist with a love of pre-1955 jazz, and my mother was a devotee of classic Broadway. These two major influences aroused in me a love of 20's jazz, 30's big band, and anything by Rodgers and Hart, Irving Berlin, Jerome Kern and occasionally Cole Porter (I could write another chapter about *him*). At an early age I was introduced to Ella, Sarah, Helen Forrest, Artie Shaw, Benny Goodman, Louis Armstrong and his Hot Five, Django Reinhardt, Bix Beiderbecke, Judy Garland, Bing Crosby and, fatefully, Mr. Sinatra.

The first time I encountered him was my mother's rented-VHS copy of *Guys and Dolls*. (We rented the VCR, too.) The tape unspooled. Mr. Sinatra was clearly handsome. But he didn't seem to be much of an actor. And I distinctly remember thinking he was sloppy.

The first of his records I bought was *Frank Sinatra: Live at the Sands*. By that time I was well aware of his art of "back-phrasing." But to my ear, Sinatra was falling off the back of the song entirely. I much preferred Crosby, who had a cleaner, clearer and, as far as I was concerned, SEXIER delivery. (And Crosby was a *great* actor. I'd been in love with him ever since my mother first rented *Blue Skies*).

Even though conventional wisdom has it that Sinatra is the King of Phrasing, I have always felt, even before I became an opinionated professional, that his "phrasing" completely ignored true musicality and the meaning of the words. And the boozy, slightly under-pitch quality he "perfected" late in his career wore me even thinner.

I appreciate that his voice had character and age and a world-weariness that people seemed to connect to. But in my heart of hearts, I think he was popular more for his vibe and lifestyle than his musicianship. I don't know who decided that the magic was in his phrasing. It most certainly wasn't me.

JAMES TAYLOR

by Ryan McGee

Ahem…

Hi, my name is Ryan.

Hi, Ryan.

I'm from North Carolina. And I hate James Taylor.

And I'm okay with it. Even if everyone around me in nearly every town I've ever lived in has been appalled by it. They react as if I've committed Carolina blasphemy, like pulling the feathers off Richard Petty's cowboy hat, or throwing a tomato at Dean Smith.

I just don't buy JT. I think his music is slow, plinky, and more than a little whiny. I used to try to be diplomatic about it. *Look, it's nothing personal,* I'd say. *It's just not for me.*

But over the years, my dislike has grown into downright hatred. Because I have been targeted, insulted, even bullied by Taylor-lovers: deranged superfans with a vastly greater intensity than the watery music they profess to love. For 43 years, these JT-culties have gone out of their way to punish me, bludgeoning my eardrums with endless renditions of his "Greatest Hits." And then - the coup de grace - they unsheath their acoustic weapons, and warble through their painful cover versions: tributes to their own enslavement.

I'm convinced that they want to brainwash me. It's like the old guy I ran into last month, who, while waiting with me in the Jiffy Lube lobby, spent an hour trying to convince me of the nutritional value of a potted meat diet. It didn't work, even as he increased his volume. Well, the JT fans haven't convinced me either, even as they've increased the volume of his music. Instead, they've just incubated my issues to a boil.

So, now it's my turn. *You've Got A Friend?* At a wedding? Really? Have you listened to the lyrics? The main character isn't in love. If anything, he's stuck in the "friend zone." And you do know that's actually a Carole King song, right?

No one really knows where he's from, by the way. Even though everyone thinks they do. They're practically in a bunkhouse stampede to claim him as their own. But largely, the reasons they do are completely off base.

Bostonians claim Taylor as theirs because he was born there. They even let him sing on the field at Fenway Park during the World Series. But he moved out of Boston when he was three years old. He's about as Bostonian as one of those Hollywood actors, braying his way through a bad *shipyahd* accent in *The Departed*.

North Carolinians claim him, too - and sure, he did grow up in Chapel Hill. But juuuust when it was time to go to high school... it was back to Massachusetts for Jimmy: shipped off to the tony Milton Academy. A far cry from tar heel country.

As I write this today, I'm in Southern California. Three different people have asked me what I'm working on. (That's how they do in LA.) Upon learning, they've said, "Oh, James *Taylor*? He's *from* here." No, dammit, he's not.

And no one - *no one* - knows what "Fire And Rain" is about. But once again, everyone thinks they do. In college, my drunk friends would throw the song into the boom box, cry, and say it was about a plane crash that killed his band. Wrong. After college, my drunk coworkers would throw the song onto the CD player, cry, point to some old house, and say that's where his girlfriend hung herself, so he wrote the song about her. Wrong again.

And how did he get into the Rock and Roll Hall of Fame? More distressingly, how did he get in way back in 2000. That's a year before Aerosmith, two years before Tom Petty, and - get this - *three years before AC/DC?* Is there a "Strumming Softly On The Delta House Stairs" wing of the Hall of Fame I don't know about?

So, to the chagrin of my fellow Carolinians, my resistance holds firm. In the end, there is one hard, fast truth that I know about the James Taylor musical experience. For I, too, have seen fire and rain. And you know what happens? It all mixes together to create a pile of wet, smoldering nothing.

IGOR STRAVINSKY

by Seth Morgulas

Lean and hungry as a commissar of the late Soviet, they sit in prime orchestra seats at Avery Fisher, wearing black. They stroke their chins appreciatively, as if the slightest indication of hostility could result in a trip to the gulag. And these are merely the casual fans. Dotting their ranks are the orthodox: lumpy tweed jackets, with the actual score spread across their laps, scrupulously parsing every last e-flat to ensure that the fourth bassoonist has not perhaps been a trifle off-key during the 289th measure.

During the *intermezzo* the lobby conversation ranges from the grudgingly positive (the expressive brilliance of the latest Mark Rothko exhibit) to the haughtily negative (the banal proles, nestled somewhere in filthier corners of the city, eating Swanson TV dinners to the pedestrian tones of *I Quattro Stagione*).

In the 1970s, twenty-five cents was a lot of money to a kid. Every night dinner rolled around, and with it, the opportunity to earn purchasing power for at least a pack of gum. My father, a lawyer by trade (but a composer at heart) would offer ten cents or more, depending on the level of difficulty, to Name That Composer. Double or nothing for the specific piece of music.

Mozart, generally, wasn't worth much – too simple. Bruckner or Mahler could be worth up 50 cents. Cousin Korngold or Schoenberg perhaps 75 cents. But oh, did the frenetic, ear-piercing, drunken wail of waterboarded tapirs howling those Stravinsky opuses pay.

To this day I am shocked that my father never recognized the tonal similarities between Stravinsky and the atrocious raping of cello strings I performed for 45 minutes every night from second through tenth grade. He confidently assured me that - one day! - I would understand the brilliant tonal complexities emanating from Stravinsky's music. Needless to say, my epiphany - my *anagnorisis*, if you will - never came. I will never understand, nor will I ever want to listen to, Igor Stravinsky.

I credit the perseverance of his reputation to one of the prime symptoms of intellectualism: praising works purely because nobody else likes them.

PEARL JAM

by Alicia Biggart

1994 was the year that I decided my ticket into the popular crowd was popular music. We had just moved to Oyster Bay, and my awkward twelve-year-old self was hyperaware of my outsider status. I decided to fake a personality that I thought my new classmates would find interesting. I decided that Pearl Jam would play a pivotal role.

My Christmas list that year consisted only of one request: Pearl Jam's *Vitalogy*. Despite knowing nothing about the band, the album, or even the genre of music, I was sure that my cool factor would be elevated as soon as I was seen rocking out to PJ on my Discman. It never occurred to me that I might not actually *like* the band. That never even crossed my mind. I was all in, fully committed to my new favorite band before hearing a note.

Christmas morning came, and to my surprise I received what seemed like every piece of Pearl Jam memorabilia ever made. My mother had provided hats, shirts, stickers, CD's, cassettes, and pins. I was officially ready to hear my new favorite band.

Therein lay the problem.

The lyrics were too dark and Eddie Vedder was way too old and the whole, you know, *image* was just a bit much for my tween brain to handle. Maybe it was just the *Vitalogy* of it all: the fact that they had already twisted inward, darkening into atonality, rebelling against their own fame. But none of that computed at the time. All I knew was that this "music" sounded like noise; feedback; sadness. The agonized wail of a catastrophically miscalculated Christmas list.

I tried to make it work, I really did. I tried listening to the music with the memorabilia *on*. Still nothing. I silently pivoted, mourning the Christmas gifts I should have requested. I even wore the memorabilia around the house for a few weeks, in a stoic attempt to prevent my mother from figuring out how much money she had wasted.

Eventually, I quietly sneaked back to my *Lion King* soundtrack, snuggling back into my pastel polo shirts.

If the day ever comes when I can listen to Pearl Jam music objectively, I might just have a change of heart. But to this day, they simply remind me of my sad, twelve-year-old, Christmas-free self.

RICHARD WAGNER

by Michelle Brazier

Dear Herr Richard Wagner,

Just because you could write a fifteen-hour opera cycle that takes four days to perform does not mean you had to do it. Have you any idea how much pain and suffering you have caused countless musicians, spouses of opera lovers, and those of us who love the opera from the inside out? Do you have even the slightest shred of pity for those of us who cannot embrace your genius, your revolutionary impact on opera, your insane magnitude?

I have spent my fair share of time and money in the balcony at *The Metropolitan Opera*. I have yet to survive *The Ring*.

I have tried it in pieces. *Die Walküre,* with its buxom, helmeted ladies was supposed to be my gateway drug. It didn't take. Then *Siegfried:* I remember thinking, maybe the sword will draw me in. No dice.

I have played concert-version excerpts from your other operas – *Lohengrin, Dutchman, Tannhäuser, Tristan* – sweating in the violin section, desperately clambering up your wall of notes. These experiences did not endear me to you any more than my visits to the balcony. It is the testosterone-fueled mightiness of your endeavors – from the mythology to the breathless staging of the end of the world – that shuts me down completely. How much self-absorption, hero worship, and God complex can a normal person really take?

If I devoted myself to you, gave up my life as I know it, and made a study of your oeuvre; if I got inside your music, and found empathy for your (supposedly) universal characters (with whom I can only muster the thinnest connection, sigh), I might be able to understand your musical world. I may even grudgingly be able to say, "OK. I like it." But I will forever feel outside of the cult of opera for not being able to embrace you without this effort. For that, I cannot forgive you.

But I must say, as a postscript: I AM a fan of the Wagner tuba. Perhaps that shall be the path towards my redemption.

Sincerely,

Michelle

BOB MARLEY

by Alex Buono

In 1991, I left the grungy Pacific Northwest for the palm tree-lined fantasy world of La-La land as I started my freshman year at the University of Southern California. My entire wardrobe at the time consisted of variations on plaid flannel and puffy vests. But I was determined to shed my dull, suburban high school persona, and immediately adopt a new SoCal identity.

By sheer luck, my dorm-mate happened to be the most cliché (and therefore perfect) model for me: a tow-headed surfer kid from San Juan Capistrano. His name was Rick.

Rick was instantly the coolest guy I had ever met. He had long, sun-bleached hair, drove a rag-top Jeep CJ-7, and spoke in that unmistakable SoCal cadence. He was basically a real-life Jeff Spicoli. Best of all, Rick had great taste in music, rescuing me from the depressing angst of Vedder and Cobain, with the warm, island stylings of that guru of *broheim*-osity: Bob Marley.

By winter break I had grown out my hair and traded my REI for tie-dye. I was a hacky-sack-playing, puka-shell-wearing, drumcircler, in perpetual need of a shower, like so many other white suburban kids on campus.

And Bob Marley was our official soundtrack. It mattered little that none of us had any idea what a "buffalo soldier" was, nor a clue about the first tenet of Rastafarianism, nor any inkling of life in Trenchtown. "Bob Marley" was an instant lifestyle prescription: a counter-culture icon who was *just* non-threatening enough to embrace without actually embracing anything political. I could just chill out to the hypnotic reggae beat, adopt the faintest Cali-Jamaican accent, and pretend that I knew how to surf.

After Christmas break, I was stunned to discover that Rick was not returning to USC. In truth, I learned that Rick had dropped out after the first month of classes, *ergo,* had been basically free-loading in my dorm room for the entire fall semester.

I tried to keep the incense burning in Rick's absence. But nothing seemed the same. Least of all, Bob Marley. As the reggae-spell lifted, I looked in the mirror and thought, "*Who the hell am I trying to be?*" Even worse: "*What the hell am I listening to??*"

Bear in mind: this is the same year that Pearl Jam's *Ten* and Nirvana's *Nevermind* albums launched the grunge explosion. Next to those fiery voices, Bob Marley might as well have been Mr. Rogers. That soft reggae beat, that smiling benevolent face, forever

THERE, I SAID IT

draped by a sun-flared cannabis-haze...and those polite, radio-friendly lyrics, that even my grandmother could hum along to:

"*Rise up this morning / Smile at the rising sun / Three little birds / Pitch by my doorstep...*"

What kind of soundtrack for youth in revolt was this?!

It's almost twenty years later, and while I recognize Bob Marley's place in music history, I still don't get it. Are these songs of political defiance? Or should I be drinking a margarita? The answer seems to be: both! He is the music world's version of cinema's embarrassing "magical black man" archetype – that safe, stock black character who comes to the aid of the white protagonist with sage wisdom and mystical powers: a malleable symbol wrapped in nursery rhymes. In short, he is the Morgan Freeman of music – right down to Mr. Freeman's Sesame Street roots.

Maybe the real Bob Marley deserved better than this. Maybe he was unfairly co-opted into becoming a commercialized pop-reggae sensation by Chris Blackwell, the British record producer and founder of Island Records. Blackwell had been searching for a cipher with the right image to fuse the Jamaican sound with the rebellious impulse of British rock music. Bob Marley had the right look at the right time.

In the end, maybe Bob would have preferred his musical legacy to echo his charged opinions about political strife in Jamaica, or the injustice of South African apartheid, or even his deep embrace of the Rastafari movement. Instead, we're left with the "House of Marley" line of audio accessories, including the "We Be Jammin' Bluetooth Audio Speaker" and the "Get Up Stand Up Digital Audio System." Head on over to www.drinkmarley.com for a case of "Marley Mellow Mood" decaffeinated ice teas! Or try www.marleynaturalshop.com for a full line of Marley body lotions along with a $40 "Positive Vibrations" aromatherapy candle. You get the picture.

And that's my beef with "Bob Marley": he's a phony. There, I said it. Bob the Man may have been an inspiring, deep-thinking human being. But Bob the Musical Legend is about as authentic as a Red Stripe beer commercial. He's a tourism ad for a Caribbean cruise, and the official mascot of ten thousand frat guys from the Midwest doing beer-bongs in Bob Marley-branded rasta-caps.

The irony is, after spending two decades avoiding the type of event that might have Bob Marley on the playlist (usually right after Jimmy Buffet or Garth Brooks – don't get me started on those guys), Bob Marley's music made a grand re-entrance into my life, this time in a vastly more appropriate, if no less ear-wormingly vexing way: it was by far the best music to help rock my newborn baby to sleep.

BOB DYLAN

by Joshua Shelov

OK so Bob Dylan.

As I mentioned in the introduction, this is not a hate book. This is a series of personal confessions. This essay is not about Bob Dylan: it's about me, and my attempt to understand why I have never in my life, not for a single three-minute stretch of his music, loved Bob Dylan.

The irony here is thick. I am the eldest child of two boomers, both of them no-nukes hippie-peaceniks. My taste was born in their record collection, a steady spin of not just '60s music but '60s *folk* music. My dad literally PLAYED THE BANJO. To have grown up in a family that loved Pete Seeger and Joan Baez and Simon and Garfunkel and Cat Stevens and Tom Lehrer, brainy/soulful issues-oriented singer-songwriters who hoisted their lyrics like picket signs, musicians I continue to love to this day...I mean, it is downright bizarre that I have never gone through a single legit Bob Dylan phase.

But it's true. He has kept me at an unrelenting distance. And I, in turn, him.

60

Why?

Well, look, it ain't complicated. It starts and ends with the Occam's Razor knock against Bob Dylan, which is that he is a flat-out terrible singer. A drowning cat. A mewling goat. The pitiful creature Gollum, straining against a leash of elvish rope.

That's pretty much it. I don't like Bob Dylan because he doesn't sing well.

But OK, fine, since you've got me thinking about this, I guess it goes a little bit deeper than that.

Let me break it down into two sub-categories. The first one being: my ears.

My ears are Beatles ears. They are melody ears, harmony ears. On the great sugar-salt spectrum of rock 'n' roll appreciation, I am sugar all the way. Even within the friendly confines of the Beatles oeuvre, I'm inclined towards the Paul stuff, which is of course not merely sweet but like walking-past-the-Cinnabon sweet. I like me some John and George, sure (especially *You've Got To Hide Your Love Away*), but for my money the height of the Beatles reputation rests on Paul's Greatest Hits: *Yesterday, Eleanor Rigby, Blackbird, Penny Lane, Michelle, The Fool On The Hill, For No One, Fixing A Hole...*

the epicenter of my taste is the Pauliest of the Paul stuff, the songs where George Martin's layering-on of strings feels not treacly but perfect.

So, these are the ears that "HOOOWWWWWW does it FEEEEUUUUHHHLLL" is landing on.

The second, more complicated factor, is about the *type* of terrible singer Bob Dylan is.

It's that he kind of *wants* to be terrible.

The way I hear it, Dylan's famously contrarian attitude contorts his singing voice to be worse than it actually is. Which was not very good to begin with.

He's kind of *trying* to suck. I think that's a big part of my problem.

Now, for what it's worth, I think his trying-to-suck is also a significant part of his appeal. When he sings, Bob Dylan is kind of communicating to his fans, *fuck you for listening.* And people - O, ye legion of Dylanites - you lap that shit up. You love Dylan's whole Garbo thing, the way he gave the finger to his loyal folkies by plugging in at the Newport Folk Festival. You love giving him your love, and you love him recoiling from your love.

Now look, I'm all about an artist experimenting, growing, re-fusing to rest on his laurels. As an isolated incident, I applaud Dy-lan for ditching acoustic at the height of his Acoustic Godhead pe-riod. But with Dylan, there's something deeper at work. There's a *personal* elusiveness that crosses over into affront: a contempt for anyone and everyone around him. You know what I'm talking about. It's that willful, *you're not allowed to know me, no one can know me, I'm going to stay out of sight not only artistically, but physically, emotionally.* And I think that this DNA-level perpetual *fuck you* is the thing that pushes me away, much more than, say, other non-melodically-gifted singers like Springsteen and Tom Waits and Leonard Cohen, R.I.P.

Cohen is a perfect counter-example. He can't sing particular-ly well. He's kind of gravelly and workmanlike and flat. But he is *exceedingly* clear. Cohen spends years honing his hyper-literate, po-etic lyrics. And when he sings, *you are damn well going to understand those lyrics.*

Cohen's clarity is an aperture. It lets you in. A Leonard Cohen song is a strange, mysterious journey. But you are on the train with him.

I've been trying to climb aboard the Bob Dylan train forever. I've turned on *Blood on the Tracks* and *Highway 61 Revisisted,* uninterrupted, good sound system. I have stood on the platform and waited, ticket in hand.

But when that train starts pulling in - when Bob Dylan starts singing - I swear to God I feel like the conductor is literally kicking me, beating me back onto the platform.

onceuponatimeyoudressedsofine threwthebumsadimeinyourprime

Dylan is probably the most respected lyricist of the 20th century. He has written lyrics that have literally been deemed worthy of the Nobel Prize in Literature.

And yet with his performance, he seems determined to obscure them. He stabs at them, slashes at them, throws them away.

I don't want my favorite artists' messages spelled out. I love ambiguity. All I want is what they're going after. I'm just happy to be along for the ride.

But with Bob Dylan, it's like...well, off he goes, I guess.

I'm ditched. Back at the station.

And I'm like fine, dude, whatever. Be that way.

LED ZEPPELIN

by Jaclyn Reindorf Savolainen

It wasn't until I was well into adulthood that I could identify Led Zeppelin by ear. It happened almost unconsciously. Every time one of their songs came on the radio, or on my husband's iPod, after a minute or so (or maybe more - their songs are awfully long), I would feel a strong, clear, urgent need:

Make it stop.

You know how you can have a subtle irritation and you can't even put your finger on the source? *Why am I feeling agitated? Why is my blood pressure rising? Why am I ANGRY?* It can take a little while before you even notice that it's happening. But then it grows and grows until your conscious mind interrupts and tells you precisely what's been bothering you.

It's Led Zeppelin. Every time.

Maybe it's because I've never done drugs. Maybe it's because I've never seen them live. Maybe it's because I've never seen them live while I was doing drugs. Maybe I'm too much of a feminist to appreciate *this much* bombastic machismo. Or maybe I just missed

65

them: I wasn't even out of diapers when they were busy turning the 70s into THE SEVENTIES.

I will grant that there is complexity in their arrangements. I can hear that their instrumentation is tight, and it's clear the band members had a musical chemistry with each other. It's very cool to play an electric guitar with a violin bow (although Jimmy Page was not the first to do so). I also acknowledge that Led Zeppelin re-imagined and reworked the Blues, and they seem to have drawn from a broad foundation of musical disciplines. But what strikes me as their most impressive achievement is setting the style for an era. They offered music fans a way forward, out of the sixties, and, later, a potent counterargument to disco.

I get all that.

I just don't see how people actually *liked* what they had to of-fer. The shrill wailing/screaming/singing is grating. I don't under-stand their lyrics: when I read them, they seem like random collec-tions of phrases, vaguely mystical, blatantly sexual, making an ob-vious attempt at poetry, but ultimately landing in the valley of the ridiculous.

And why is soft LOUD soft LOUD a desirable dynamic? Why is aural dissonance appealing? What emotional state benefits from frenetic energy? Why celebrate the fact that the band spawned an era of ear-splitting heavy metal groups?

But most of all, and most relevant to me, why must the guitar riffs (which are impressive at first) repeat and repeat and repeat and repeat and repeat and repeat and ... OH, MY GOD:

MAKE IT STOP.

A brief postscript. When I was in elementary school, I had my first kiss at a roller rink, during a slow dance to "Stairway to Heaven." It became "our song."

Only much later did I realize that I truly disliked our song. The boy went on to become an Orthodox Jew. I rest my case.

AL GREEN

by Leslie DiNicola

As a professional musician - and a woman - I'm *really* not supposed to admit this. But in the spirit of coming clean, I can honestly say that from the depths of my (apparently) cold, hard soul, I just don't get the obsession with Al Green.

It's not that I'm heartless. Give me Marvin, Otis, Sam, or Solomon any day. But if you take me back to your place after a midnight stroll, pour a couple glasses of wine, and put on Al Green, all you'll see when you turn around is a Road-Runner-esque puff of white smoke.

Over the years, I have tried to figure out the source of my inherent aversion to the undeniably smooth King of Soul. After a period of deep contemplation, I believe I can finally pin it down to one indisputable factor. A person, actually. Jared Harrington.

Oh, Jared Harrington. The mysterious, dark-haired, blue-eyed, new kid in school from the wrong side of town. There were two things I found instantly irresistible about Jared Harrington. One was the way he unassumingly grazed through the halls of our high school, observing everyone and everything with the quiet confidence and seductive grin of a young Christian Slater in *Heathers*.

Second, he had a car.

The day I found out Jared Harrington was "into me" was the single greatest day of my naïve adolescent life. After days of flirting and playing hard-to-get, in exact accordance with the rules of my November issue of *Cosmo Girl*, Jared Harrington Asked Me Out. He picked me up in his navy blue '86 Ford Bronco (we lived in Texas), and, within the first hour of our first date, I knew this was no ordinary high school romance. We didn't have dinner at Chili's. We didn't share Red Vines at the AMC while watching *City Of Angels*. No. Jared Harrington picked up tacos at a drive-thru, took me downtown to an underground rock concert, and snuck me into a seedy bar called The Slip Inn for a round of whiskey sours. It's safe to say I was in love.

Jared Harrington's mom worked late on weeknights. So, after that first romantic outing, most of our "dates" consisted of him throwing acorns at my bedroom window, helping me climb out and down via the roof over the garage, and heading over to his place. I'll be writing another article later using this same exact story to explain when and how I learned the difference between true love and a booty call. In the meantime, let's get back to the Reverend Al Green.

It was a Wednesday night. It was cold and raining. We had just arrived at his house and kicked off our shoes when he walked over to his turntable. As I shivered and casually tried to tousle my wet hair before he turned back around, I thought to myself: what was he going to put on? Was he about to fulfill my dreams of losing my virginity to Patrick Swayze under the sweet serenade of "These Arms Of Mine"? (No '90s girl can resist the killer combo of Swayze and Redding. The brainwashing starts at birth.)

And then, just like that, Jared Harrington did it. He dropped the needle and out from the crackling speakers came the unmistakable horn intro of "Let's Stay Together." Maybe it was too obvious a move. Maybe it was the added cheesiness of the rain and boxed wine. Maybe it was his odd misjudgment of the situation: had we fallen madly in love, broken up, reconciled, and were about to have make-up sex, all within the time it took us to drive from Shakey's to his house? Or do I just have freakishly steady knees, and a giant chunk of ice where my heart should be?

I'll never really know. But one thing is certain: I walked out on Jared Harrington that night. And sixteen years later, I still can't get into Al Green.

BRUCE SPRINGSTEEN

by Christine Caddick

I love music. I appreciate music. I respect music. Pick any genre and I'll give you my favorite artist and favorite song. Look at my iPod: Dinah Washington. Daddy Yankee. Bonnie Raitt. LLCool J. The Manhattan Transfer. Invite me to a concert and I'll go, even if I've never heard of the artist, just for the opportunity to experience live music. I can say with conviction that every concert experience since my very first one (1981, Crystal Gayle, apologies) was tremendous.

With one exception. Bruce Springsteen.

It was the summer of 2009. My best friend declared: "Bruce Springsteen is going to be in Hartford and we are making ourselves go." Notice her use of the word 'making.' We were both baffled by the popularity of Bruce Springsteen. But our hearts, at the time, were open. We saw *ourselves*, and not Bruce - at least potentially - as the problem.

Mind you, it's not just that I don't get Bruce. I *can't stand* Bruce. Mention his name and I cringe. The soul patch and angry under-bite never did it for me. I actually felt sorry for Courteney

Cox when she got pulled on stage during the "Dancing in the Dark" video. To my ears, every Springsteen song sounds exactly the same. And his voice, a beacon of truth for so many, only makes me crave a lozenge.

One fan shed some light on the Springsteen phenomenon for me. He admitted that he once shared my views. But then he experienced The Boss live in concert. And he was instantly transformed into a groupie.

That's it, I thought. Going to a Boss Show will answer all of my questions. It will fill this existential void.

Back to August, 2009. My friend and I agreed to approach the concert from a place of hope. Like young Catholics approaching the Vatican, we prepared ourselves not only for education, but enlightenment.

And then, there we were.

Bruce himself comes onstage to a deafening ovation. *Here it comes,* I thought. *The transformative moment we've been waitin-*

"I'm ready to go." said my friend.

We were two songs in.

She stared at me, not in any way kidding.

No, I said, gently: understanding, but firm. I convinced her to stay, at least for a little while longer, with one argument. It had to get better.

We would repeat this exchange six more times throughout the concert. 'Let's go." 'Not yet.'

Springsteen is a gifted musician, and he gives 100%. But his songs, I'm sorry, are flat with repetitive melodies. His voice is a growl, at best. Unless it's a serious song, which he indicates by jutting out his chin and speak-singing the lyrics. And the factory closes down and the girl runs away and Bobby goes off to war.

The stories rolled by, and my friend and I felt nothing after nothing after nothing. Yet somehow, his aura had turned the crowd around us into a devoted, weeping mass of humanity. They knew every word. They held up hand-painted signs. They glowed in their profound love.

After two and a half hours, it just hadn't gotten better. More troubles lay ahead: more layoffs and plant closings and trouble down by the river. And so my friend and I departed, with Bruce and his fans still going strong.

We left more confused than when we arrived, feeling a strange pity for all of his fans, who obviously just didn't know any better. We wanted to like Bruce, we really did. We drove for awhile in silence. Then my friend turned to me and said, "What concert were those people listening to?"

BARBRA STREISAND

by Marc Chalpin

First, the indisputable facts. Barbra Streisand is one of the most successful singers of all time. She has sold over 71.5 million records in the US, and more than double that worldwide. She's had over 30 top-ten albums, and has even crossed over, with smashing success, into film, where she won a Best Actress Oscar for *Funny Girl.*

Therefore, when I think of Barbra Streisand, four words come to mind:

I don't get it.

Let's go back to my childhood.

My older sister is a huge Streisand fan. Growing up, she would refer to Streisand as the second-best singer of all time, listing Judy Garland as number one. Being involuntarily subjected to Streisand's music, as covered and reinterpreted by my sister, may very well be a significant factor herein.

Despite my sister's claims, there are simply so many singers I find better than Streisand that to claim she is the second best of all time is mindboggling. While many of her songs are well-known and popular, I would argue that any singer that could carry a tune could have made those songs hits.

But here is the crux of the matter.

I always get the feeling that Streisand feels she's almost too good to perform—that when she performs, it's like she's granting her audience an audience.

Compare that to Paul McCartney, who would, by the numbers, be in every position to consider himself superior not only to his audience, but to the entire human race. Paul conveys none of this scoffiness. To cite only one example I happened to witness personally, I once saw Sir Paul in attendance at a Yankee game. A Beatles' song came on the speaker, and McCartney was caught on the big screen singing along like half the fans in the Stadium. He smiled happily, as delighted as the crowd. He got a massive, *kindred,* ovation.

I would ask you to imagine Barbra Streisand in that same scene. First of all, the idea of her sitting open-air, in the stadium, among the hoi polloi, is all but unimaginable. The only way Babs enters the stadium is insulated from the people: limo-to-luxury box. And if some keen-eyed PA jockey happened to spot her, through the tinted glass? And happened to play one of Babs's greatest hits, while a game camera, screwing on its longest lens, caught her unawares? Putting her, and her music, on the telecast, together? Is there the slightest chance that she would do anything but recoil? From her fans, from her music, from herself?

Sorry, Babs. I'm out.

JOHN LENNON

by Steve J. Rogers

I submit to you that John Lennon is overrated.

Not as the heart, soul, and rebellious spirit of the Beatles, mind you. Nor does he have many peers as a writer of songs of socio-political impact.

But I must say that his solo output tends to place Lennon on a pedestal that he just doesn't belong on.

His tragic murder on December 8th, 1980 has a lot to do with it: probably everything to do with it. The "Lennon as martyr" storyline elevated his stature to a level that even John himself would scoff at. Much of the thinking that placed Lennon ahead of the rest of the Beatles in terms of artistic vision was hatched during this emotional, post-assassination period, most notably Philip Norman's *Shout!,* a driving force behind the shaping of the Lennon Legend.

Of course we'll never know what Lennon could have given us, had he not been coldly murdered nearly a month after *Double Fantasy's* release. But if one simply takes a look at Lennon's decade of solo work up to that point, it is hard to say that it is all-time classic stuff. And the underlying reason for the meandering quality of the work is Lennon's unfocused and lazy nature, an attitude that even goes back to his heyday with the Fab Four.

Sure, there is enough solid solo material to fill a Greatest Hits album. "Instant Karma" and "Happy X-Mas" are kept in classic rock rotation with good reason. And "Imagine" is a work of pure magic, difficult to criticize on any level. But those three songs feel like anomalies, in an otherwise baffling decade of work. I mean, *man*, Lennon sure gave us an awful lot of "experimental" music that, let's face it, was much more avant garbage than avant garde (though considering Lennon's sense of humor, there is a small possibility that it all could have been a massive rib). Throw in an uninspired album of cover songs, made purely to satisfy a lawsuit, and you're just not looking at much besides some post-Beatles fumes.

Let's face it: all four Beatles could have retired in 1970, never to write another lick of music, and they would have owed us nothing. But the work we got from Lennon...I'm just saying...is perhaps not everything it has been cracked up to be.

COUNTING CROWS

by Julian Sheppard

The worst part is I only know that one damn song.

So I feel almost ashamed at my loathing, like I heard some-one cough in an elevator and decided they had pneumonia. But if someone coughs in your face, repeatedly, and no matter where you turn, they're coughing in your face, and the worst part is other people, your friends who say, "Oh no, I don't mind being coughed on, actually I kinda like it, the cough's really *catchy*!" ... well, you can't really help but think either everyone is else is flat-out crazy... or you're wrong.

Maybe it wasn't even the song, not even the dumb lyrics, the bleating chorus, the banal music, the vaguely referential self-aware *we're so smart* referencing of Dylan with "Mr. Jonnnneeessssss and meeeeeeeeee."

Or maybe it's the name of the band. It's the kind of name you give your band in 10th grade ("Man, *counting crows,* it sounds totally Native American, but like, not!") and jettison when you become an adult.

Maybe it isn't even all that.

Maybe it's the dreads.

Just because you have dreadlocks doesn't make you sound any less like a third-rate bat mitzvah band, or take away that your last name is Duritz and your parents probably drove a Volkswagen and you were always the last one picked in soccer and – I can't even hear how much I hate the song because I can't get out of my head how much I hate *looking* at it.

So do I just hate the *video*? Is that it? Do I hate Counting Crows and Adam Duritz because he's a nice Jewish boy who grew dreadlocks and is what I am not, a star, internationally known to rock the microphone? Is it just jealousy that he worked hard and became what I wished I was when I was 13, the lead singer of a rock-n-roll band?

I don't hate "Mr. Jones." I don't hate Counting Crows. I hate me. I need to dig deeper, get past the initial revulsion – somewhere, like on the third album, maybe the fourth track, there must be a song that I wouldn't hate. Maybe not love, but not hate. It's me, not them. For god's sake, it's just one song.

I had stopped thinking about them for awhile, after their omnipresent heyday. But apparently they've been recording and touring for years. They were nominated for an Oscar, I guess? They've got a large and loyal following. People love Counting Crows. I decided to do a bit of googling, checking out their history, discography, impressive longevity, and – oh wait.

I don't just know that one song. I also know "Round Here."

That song's even *worse*.

It sounds like someone tortured an animal, recorded it, and then played it back too slowly. I hate that song so much I blocked it out of my memory. I hate that song more then I hate myself.

So it wasn't just a cough. They're the flu.

PAUL MCCARTNEY

by Patti Weiser

When I was ten, my family went on a cross-country camping trip. My mom, dad, brother, sister and I loaded up the family truckster with enough coolers of mom's frozen best to cover our three-week journey. Pillows, books, sleeping bags, guitar.

On that trip I wrote my first song, aptly named for our destination: "California." It went something like this:

"California, California, California, California, California..."

Within seconds, the whole family knew it by heart. It was awesome.

Flash forward. I'm now 30. Paul McCartney is touring, and my sister gets tickets for me and our mom at the Cap Center in D.C. That night he sang a song called "Driving Rain" ("one, two, three, four, five, let's go for a drive...")

About halfway through that song, I remember getting angry and thinking, "My California song is easily as good as this. But just because this guy happened to be a Beatle, he's up on stage, and I'm in the back row squinting to see him."

I don't dispute the greatness of the Beatles. But - really - "Driving Rain?" Really? How do you spell a word that sounds like a Yiddish mixture of ugh and yuck and ick?

And to be honest, I really don't even like his voice. Did he hurt his nose? Kind of a desperate wail sound, no? As if he were permanently saying, "Please come back, John!"

I feel like I'm defaming the dead at the funeral. And yet I must speak from the heart. You were a Beatle! C'mon! You can't expect people to just accept "Driving Rain" or your insufferable "Wonderful Christmastime" nonsense or [insert literally any Wings song].

A Beatle shouldn't be allowed to get away with writing something any child in a truckster could. Maybe that, then, is the lesson. We all have songs in us. And you don't have to be a Beatle to write or sing or shine.

But apparently you do have to be a Beatle for people to fork over top dollar to hear you sing pure cheese at the Cap Center. Do us a favor, Paul, leave the fluff to us. *"California, California, California..."*

JAMES TAYLOR, vol. 2

by Jacqui Robbins

Dear James Taylor,

It's not you; it's me. I know that. You're a musical icon, an American legend, a philanthropist, a lover. I am a 42-year-old mother who gave up piano in 11th grade and is encouraged to lip sync at L'Chaim Rest Home Family Mitzvah Project Sing-Alongs.

But here it is: I cannot see, given the vast and amazing smorgasbord of music created since Gregorians chanted, why anyone would choose to listen to you. On purpose. (I completely understand people enduring you involuntarily, i.e. in the aisles of a Walmart, or subjected to their drunk uncle Frank who used to have a band and holy God he just broke out into *Sweet Baby James*.)

I can confess all this to you this because you are so kind, so earnest, so good. I hate myself for hating you. But you will forgive me. You've probably already forgiven me. And that's the problem. Your songs are too nice, too perfectly folksy. They're that Hallmark card you buy as a joke and give to someone ironically. They make one snort.

I'll be honest: these sentiments may stem mostly from my ninth-grade graduation, when we were forced to stand sweltering in white dresses we'd sewn ourselves and vow our eternal friendlove to one another by singing *You've Got a Friend*. Which, in my case, was a lie. I did not, at the time, have any friends. I didn't even have a partner for the graduation processional because I was too tall and there were more girls than boys so I got to march in all alone, just me and the other really tall girl in the class.

It was 1986. Music was a black celebration, a rich pageant. You could go to the alternative café in the basement of Christ Church and dance your self sweaty while Moby –– yes, that Moby, the actual Moby actually went to my high school – DJ'd. If you wanted love, Whitney would sing to you about the greatest of all. If you wanted down home Americana, Mellencamp'd bring you to a small town. And yet, there I was, skirt unhemmed because I never learned to sew, way at the back of the bleachers, trying to hit that stupid high note on "I will BEEE there, yes I will."

Great. Now in addition to feeling guilty, I will have that in my head for the rest of the day. Because here's the other thing: everyone learns your songs. They shower the people with schmaltz, and they seep into our brains, and stick. I've never willingly listened to you in my life, but damnit if I don't know that you always thought you'd see her, baby, one more time again.

Now that one's in there too. There's just a few things comin' my way this time around now...

Damn you, James Taylor. I'm sorry. But damn you.

Sincerely,

Jacqui

LEONARD COHEN

by Mark Badger

I don't get Leonard Cohen, and I think it's Jeff Buckley's fault.

Not directly, of course. But if it weren't for his (justly) renowned version of Cohen's "Hallelujah," from Buckley's phenomenal album *Grace*, I think Cohen would have remained the darling of a small group of music aesthetes, those who appreciate obscure and unapproachable music as a form of cultural superiority. (As an aside, I'm sure there are some folks who appreciate Cohen but think praise for Jeff Buckley is unwarranted. They are mistaken.)

Instead, Cohen seems to occupy the echelon of artists like Tom Waits, Neil Young, Dylan, and other artists whose songwriting outstrips their vocal ability. As you might guess, I don't get those guys either. I mean, I appreciate their influence, as well as the fact that people I respect seem to get them. But I just can't get past their inherently unmelodious voices.

Of course, this bias against non-singer songwriters has nothing to do with Cohen in particular. It's my parents' fault.

There are certain things that come with growing up in the late '70s in an overwhelmingly non-diverse Boston suburb. One of them is an 8-track player, and the other is soft rock. Not *yacht* rock, mind you (though they share DNA). I mean Neil-Diamond-Barbra-Streisand-Barry-Manilow-Karen-Carpenter soft rock. None of these artists are cool, even ironically (OK, maybe Neil Diamond). But they can all sing. So I grew up with an appreciation for music that one listens to because of - and not despite - the lead vocals.

Even though my tastes broadened considerably as I grew up, I've never really gotten over my aversion toward unpleasant vocals (see also, e.g., Bjork). But maybe it's not just that I can't stand to listen to Cohen sing. I asked a friend for his take on Leonard Cohen, and he responded, "I think he's more of a poet than a musician."

Well, there you go, I thought. I don't get poetry either.

WOLFGANG AMADEUS MOZART

by Jeff Brock

As a card-carrying member of Generation X, I blasted my kids with hours of Baby Mozart. But when I was a kid, I got dosed with the real thing. My father was a classical musician and compulsive record collector. Ergo, I was exposed to untold gobs of classical music without prior consent. My dad tended towards the big guns: Bach, Beethoven, Brahms, etc. I liked most of it OK.

With an odd exception. There was something about Mozart that always seemed too tidy, too clean, bopping along from predictable cadence to predictable cadence, like we were all supposed to be sitting there thinking "how delightful!." (Part of the problem, perhaps, was that I wasn't all that interested, temperamentally speaking, in being delighted.)

Brahms's third symphony, on the other hand, hit me like a ton of bricks, transforming me into the weird kid with a symphony in his new walkman. *Deceptive cadences!* Now we're talking. *Unpredictable resolutions in non-standard directions!* This tickled my eardrums. Even at a young age, I felt a "cry" in Brahms's work - like he was talking directly to me.

There's a bit floating around the internet with Dave Grohl railing against *American Idol,* how it's destroying music, and so on. I wonder if the same can be said of the cult of perfection that has grown up around the classical music education industry.

To me, there was always an unhealthy cult of the genius in classical instruction: either you were a prodigy, or you should quit. Mozart, of course, personifies the idea of the musical prodigy.

Mr. Grohl exhorts: "Musicians should just go to a yard sale and buy an old fucking drum set and get in their garage and just suck."

I myself definitely did a whole lot of musical sucking, as a kid. And then I started to get better. I got better by playing night after night with a bunch of 60-to-80 year old dudes at the Bird Cage Jam Session in Oakland. There wasn't much perfection going on. But those guys listened to every note you played, and cheered out loud when you did something unexpected: something even they couldn't see coming.

With Brahms, Chopin, Jaco Pastorius, Jimi Hendrix, Duke Ellington, Kurt Cobain, Thelonious Monk, John Coltrane, Wayne Shorter, and Prince (I'll stop there), there's a yearning - that 'cry' again - some kind of gut-shot, soul-laid-bare moment, where the instruments melt away and the staff, key signature, and chord change simply recede. Suddenly the musician is speaking a kind of primal language.

No doubt many have experienced this with Mozart, of course. And I'll give him this one: Itzhak Perelman's adagio in the Mozart violin concerto is one of the most linguistic, evocative, wrenching, heart-breaking pieces of fiddling I've ever heard. My man Perelman can bring it.

But for me, as a young musician, Mozart's genius, brilliance, prodigious talent, and, yes, mastery, felt porcelain.

Is perfection itself really sublime?

And after all, what did the real baby Mozart listen to? I'm betting it was baby Bach...

STEELY DAN

by Greg Raskin

This assignment reminds of nothing so much as Woody Allen's short story "A Little Louder, Please," in which the narrator first boasts of his brilliance ("Understand you are dealing with a man who knocked off *Finnegan's Wake* on the roller coaster at Coney Island ...") and then spends the rest of the story explaining how he cannot, for the life of him, understand mimes.

And so, let me set the scene.

In the late 1980s, I was a melancholy teen with a Walkman, and then a Discman. I had a penchant for making sensitive mixtapes, which never impressed the girls as much as I thought they should. Those tapes marked the beginning and end of my musical career. Music critics, much like the girls I tried to impress, greeted my creative *oeuvre* with muted indifference.

Steely Dan, on the other hand, has some serious critical *bona fides*. They have been a darling from the moment they released their first album in 1972, *Can't Buy a Thrill*. They have three albums in *Rolling Stone* magazine's Top 500. They have won numerous

Grammys, including the Album of the Year in 2001. They are in the Rock and Roll Hall of Fame.

But back to my career, if I may. The mixtapes of my yesteryear have become Spotify playlists, to which I subject the other members of my family of four, especially on long road trips. My wife appreciates them, she says. My kids put up with them. When we tire of these playlists, we listen to satellite radio.

When I hear Steely Dan, those critical-darling Hall of Famers, I change the channel immediately.

Their story is well known. Donald Fagen and Walter Becker met in 1968, as classmates at Bard College. They began writing and playing music together. Drafting others to play around them, they released seven successful albums from 1972 to 1981. They broke up for a decade or so. Then they scored a major comeback in 2001, with a Grammy-Award-winning Album of the Year, *Two Against Nature*.

Let us examine their most egregiously terrible song: "Deacon Blues" (1977). Inane lyrics about some depressed suburban guy are set to a tune that truly uninspires, with an arrangement that exquisitely showcases just how boring the melody is. About four minutes into the song, there is a saxophone solo that I really don't care about, but at least it spared me, for 45 seconds or so, from another self-indulgent verse. If you keep listening, which I forced my-self to in order to write this paragraph, more singing occurs. The song's deep insight into the human condition includes the revelato-ry observation that the University of Alabama's football team is known as the Crimson Tide.

In an interview in New Music Express in the 1970s, Donald Fagen was quoted as saying, "We don't necessarily try to communi-cate any specific thing to the listener." Mission accomplished! (Did I mention that "Deacon Blues" is seven and a half minutes long?)

Perhaps I am not mature enough to appreciate their fine jazz stylings. Critics fawn all over the Dan's session musicians - *drafted from Miles Davis's own band - ooohhh.* Maybe I'm too much of a Philistine to comprehend the virtuosity of Walter Becker's guitar playing, or the duo's Grammy-winning sound engineering. And I am clearly not intellectual enough to grasp the *sotto voce* cleverness of their lyrics ("wry, nuanced and hyper-literate," says the Hall of Fame website); nor their band name (which is famously named af-ter a sex toy -- so cheeky!).

Or perhaps they are just super-boring, ladies and gentlemen: the rock and roll equivalent of two mimes against nature.

STEVIE WONDER

by Henry Tenney

Oh Stevland Hardaway Judkins, a.k.a. Stevie Wonder, don't take this the wrong way, OK? I don't hate you. You're a real talented guy, I guess. And sure, you seem nice enough and all. It's just that... well... I don't *revere* you like everybody else seems to.

What can I say? I just don't think the sun shines out of that annoying little Melodica of yours. You'd expect I'd have company in this opinion. But I don't think I've ever heard anyone express anything less than gushing, over-the-top, superlative joy about you and your music. Never heard anyone complain about your painful, strident vocal performance in *Living for the City*. Never heard any-one who doesn't bob and smile when *Boogie On, Reggae Woman* comes on the radio for spin #5,612,992 of your seven billion daily plays. (And, if I may, "Boogie On"? Who even says that? And to a Reggae Woman, no less?)

I ask these questions because no one else will.

I mean Stevie, really, we all love our kids, but did you really have to write a song about your baby daughter *and* record her googling and blabbering for it too? And did it really have to become the single most requested song for weddings and birthdays, bachelorette parties and bat mitzvahs?

Everybody cuts you major bolts of slack. From agit-pop anarchists to Bossa Novans to Norwegian black metal growl-singers, it seems like none of them has ever spoken a bad word about you. Why? Why is the praise for you so universal, much more so than, oh, I don't know, any other musician I can think of?

People slag off on Billy Joel all the time, even on Paul Simon and James Taylor. But drop a shade bomb on old Stevland Judkins, well, I don't know what would happen. Because I've never dared try it. I expect I'd be ostracized immediately; sent to a desert island. With my luck it would be an island overflowing with copies of *Innervisions,* since it's seems to be *everybody's* Desert Island Disc.

So, I suffer you in silence for fear of losing all my friends and having a Lite-Funk Fatwa put on my head. It's lonely sometimes, having to pretend I like "Superstition" when I hear it for the quintillionth time. I'd love to save people from him, to be honest with you. I'd like to stop the sheep-like trough feed of his goo-smeared musical Wonder Bread. But no one would listen. Nobody realizes they need saving from Stevie Wonder. Clearly they can't hear me over that sickeningly chipper faux horn riff from "Sir Duke." So I'll just sit here, acting like everything is all right. Uptight. Clean outta sight.

TOM WAITS, vol. 2

by Ron Wechsler

Tom Waits is one of those artists that other artists love. Artists like Scarlett Johansson.

Oh, Tom Waits, he's my hero...his voice..it's just the epitome of soul.

No.

Otis Redding is soul. Sam Cooke. Aretha. Not some dude who sounds like shrapnel.

Tom Waits...he's just so raw and real.

Ooooh, you've got a soul patch and wear a HAT!

Look, maybe, MAYBE I'll give him that "Hallelujah" cover they used in *Shrek,* only because my kids sung it for a few days and that was cute. Wait...that's Leonard Cohen? Well, hell, Waits just lost even more credibility with me. Just because he starred in a Jim Jarmusch movie doesn't mean I have to like him. If anything, that makes his pretentiousness-quotient even worse. Quick, name three

Jim Jarmusch movies. That's right, you can't. And if you can, you need to get out of my house.

Dammit, look what's happened. Now I'm ranting about Jim Jarmusch. And it's all because of Tom Waits.

I know he was elected to the Rock and Roll Hall of Fame. And I know one of his albums is #397 on Rolling Stone's best 500 albums of all time. But I only know that because I just looked it up on Wikipedia.

Look, I work in sports. If you're only the 357th best athlete in a particular sport, I'm sorry but you're just not that great. Nobody goes around cooing about the greatness of the 357th best swimmer.

Perhaps my main issue is that Waits doesn't really sing. He's more of a "speak-singer." And I just can't endorse that methodology as a form of entertainment. Either you SPEAK or you SING. But you can't sping.

Well, you can, I guess. But I'll be damned if I call it musical talent. There simply must be a clear line between the two. Take a tip from Bruce Springsteen or Bono. These are artists who know how to stop a song, mid-song, THEN speak. THEN they return to singing.

See? There's a whole protocol here, Tom. And no amount of cigarettes, bourbon, facial hair, or crappy hats can justify you trying to blur these lines.

Hallelujah.

THE GRATEFUL DEAD

by Neil Turitz

I won't bury the lead. I don't take drugs stronger than booze. And I hate the Grateful Dead. I am fully aware that these two sentences may be fundamentally identical.

And yet, I have a story to tell.

A year or so out of college, during a quiet St. Patrick's Day celebration on the Upper West Side, I met a couple of college girls from UMass, who were passing through on their way to Philly. Their ultimate destination was a Dead show the following night. The drinks were flowing and my beer goggles were firmly in place. But the girls seemed friendly enough, and while I couldn't talk either of them into coming home with me that night, by the time we took our leave of each other, they asked me to join them on their journey.

I was 22. The adventure seemed rife with possibilities. I accepted.

It should be noted that - even at the time - I considered the Dead to be the worst rock and roll band in existence, with the possible, well-documented, exception of the Moody Blues.

But at the time, my objection to the Dead was purely academic. A road trip with two hot 19-year-old girls? I would have gone with them to Nuremberg.

The next day, I was pleased to learn that both girls were, in fact, quite attractive: the goggles I'd worn the night before hadn't been as Coke-bottle-thick as I'd feared. Off we went to Philly. On the way, we picked up another young lady who, upon getting into the car, opened an Altoid box to reveal a mass of pink pills. "Want a Ritalin?" she asked. "When you have one, and smoke a cigarette, it's a killer high." I mumbled my typical demurral.

We arrived at the Spectrum and parked. I had never wanted a drink so badly in my life. It was at this critical moment that a casual announcement was made to the car: nobody actually had any tickets. And oh by the way, the show was sold out.

The period that followed - six hours of wandering around the Spectrum parking lot, amidst a sea of shower-challenged hippies - constitutes the bulk of my sensory objection to The Grateful Dead. Never mind the shitty music: what *organization*, in all of human history, is responsible for scenes of such debased human carnage? I wandered to and fro, passing impossibly foul-smelling humans, who were happily banging on drums, passing around joints, burning utterly futile incense. Meanwhile, amateurish loudspeakers placed at various ends of the parking lot blasted bootlegs from previous Dead shows. But of course, the recordings weren't coordinated: so the net effect was two Grateful Dead songs - each of which was bad enough on its own - meeting up at odd angles in the center of my brain, trying their damnedest to create an aneurism. To top it all off, nobody was selling booze anywhere. Time stretched into eternity.

In later years, as I've recounted this story, staunch Deadheads have told me: *if you'd only gotten inside the stadium, man. To really appreciate the Dead, you have to watch them jam.* But I've never bought into that argument. To me, that's like saying, "I know you don't like this author. But you should really read the stuff he writes when it's all coming out stream of consciousness, with no rhyme, reason or point, totally unedited. Then you'll really get him."

As my parking lot nightmare wended its way towards conclusion, only the thought of some kind of magical, three-way sexual escapade kept me from assaulting a Deadhead. But of course, that fantasy fell apart when the girls proved themselves to be way too out of it when it was all over, both of them whacked out of their minds on opiates.

The ride back to New York the next day tended toward silence, interrupted only by awkwardness. Not even so much as a hug was exchanged upon my exit, on the corner of Broadway and 81st.

GOD, I hate the fucking Dead.

MACKLEMORE

by Elizabeth Jayne Liu

I want to talk about bragging. Because I do it a lot and I'm very good at it.

At any given moment, I have between three and five friends. When cornered, at least two of them will publicly admit to our friendship. This level of popularity might be overwhelming for some people, but I successfully nurture each relationship while remaining likeable and humble.

My innocent side wants to believe that I'm well-liked because others enjoy my company, but my sharp, worldly side isn't afraid to face the shallowness of people's true motivations. I'm the only person I know with a complete set of *Yo! MTV Raps* trading cards. I'm the only person I know with a custom-commissioned Tupac plush doll. And I'm also the only person I know who's collected enough tickets at Dave & Buster's to take home a Hamilton Beach blender. There are a lot of avenues to popularity, but those are probably the top three.

It also doesn't hurt that I listen to a lot of rap, which makes me an expert in life, money, boss bitches, cars, parole, and Tom Ford. Who among us doesn't need a well-rounded friend?

I've been a ride-or-die fan of rap since I was twelve, when I traded an entire summer day organizing my mother's overwhelming collection of Tupperware for enough money to buy Tupac's first album, *2Pacalypse Now*.

I'm Westside till I die, but I'll listen to anything—Freestyle, Gangsta rap, Trap, Dirty South, Old School, Underground, East Coast, Crunk, Snap, Electro rap, Alternative rap, G-Funk, Chopped and Screwed, and Breakbeat. Even when I get side-eye for bumping bullshit and my passengers ask me to roll up my window and turn down the volume, I bump loud and proud. Chief Keef's "Hate Bein' Sober" has been on repeat in my car for seven weeks: the same Chief Keef who rose to meteoric fame while on house arrest at the age of sixteen for heroin manufacture and distribution. (A sentence he served out, by the way, at his grandma's house.)

But my love for the genre ends at Macklemore.

It's not so much that his lyrical game is uninspired: forgettable pop music unconvincingly disguised as rap (which is totally true and probably the most important point). It's more that I got beef with rewarding safe and trite artists over genre-defining talent.

I won't begrudge Ben Haggerty aka Professor Macklemore aka Macklemore props for rapping about wearing thrift shop finds to a club when the popular rapper mentality is "fuck bargains, get me my Gucci." But come on. The dude is just silly and phony. And now he's silly and phony with four Grammy awards, two Billboard Music awards, AND a BET award. I just don't get it.

I stopped watching the Academy Awards in 2006 after "It's Hard Out Here for a Pimp" (from the film *Hustle and Flow)* won for Best Original Song. Three 6 Mafia performed the song minutes before they took the stage again to receive their award. It's the only Academy Award acceptance speech in history to thank both Jesus and Ludacris. I thought that nothing could ever top that moment.

When Macklemore received seven Grammy nominations in 2014, my initial reaction was, "What?"...which, coincidentally, is also the same word he repeats 31 times as his opening for "Thrift Shop." Macklemore won four awards including Best New Artist, Best Rap Album, Best Rap Performance, and Best Rap Song for "Thrift Shop."

What? What?

Now, not every rapper is a lyrical genius. When I listen to Outkast spit out braggadocious lines like "my words are diamonds dug out a mine / spit 'em, polish, look how they shine / glitter, glisten, gloss, floss," I respect rap as art, a medium comprised of words that are pulled and chopped and swirled together to tell stories and teach lessons and speak for those who have yet to find their own voice, all timed to a beat, making those words unforgettable and valuable. I learn something and I become aware of a greater human experience than just my own. It's hard to do that when the only word I can remember from an artist is, "What?"

NIRVANA

by Michael Fass

Sometimes I'm lucky enough to have long conversations with friends whose musical taste I admire. I love those talks. This is where friendships are hatched. Rare moments. Genuine sharing of our true selves with one another. Real kumbaya stuff.

Until the subject of Nirvana comes up. Then, my facial muscles contort. My breathing quickens. The eyelids tighten. I blush. I sweat. It's that moment when I realize that everyone else knows something that I don't. I don't get the joke; It's over my head; I'm out of the loop. Whatever it is, it sucks.

The thing is, I love music so much. I love rock and roll. My love is an active one. As a weekend warrior guitarist, I love to re-interpret songs I love, pour my heart and soul into them, and make them my own. I do this all the time. And when I'm not doing it, I'm thinking about it. This stuff *means* something to me.

But Nirvana? I'm feeling nothing.

Am I demographically challenged? Is my age or my background the problem? On the contrary: by the numbers, I should be the biggest Nirvana fan on the planet.

I graduated from North Miami Beach High School in 1989, two years before grunge exploded. As a high school senior, my musical taste was a mélange of hard and classic rock (Beatles, Zep, Van Halen), spiced with a pinch of cool and different (Chili Peppers, Beastie Boys), and seasoned with a few of my mom's folk heroes (Dylan, Neil Young, CSN).

Oh and: *I fucking hated every single last one of those dogshit 80s hair bands.* We're talking hate here, folks.

So far, I sound like a prime candidate for grunge-loving. Right?

So now I'm closing in on high school graduation. Mosh pits and neo-punk are starting to emerge in my peripheral vision. There are even a few proto-grunge local bands popping up, papering the occasional telephone pole. Unconsciously, I was absorbing the subtle foreshocks of the big bang to come. And I wasn't just an observer: I was a performer. My antennae were out. I had axe in fucking hand.

I was basically *designed in a fucking lab* to love Nirvana.

Then, I went off to college in Burlington, VT. This being UVM, I heard (for the first time) Blind Faith's "Can't Find My Way Home" on my very first day in the dorms. I took my first hit of "But Anyway" by Blues Traveler soon after. And I inhaled copious lungfuls of Phish, Dead, Hot Tuna. All of this stuff led me in rich directions for years. But not toward that thumping thing.

I came home to Miami for Thanksgiving, Christmas, summer break. Grunge hadn't quite been born yet, but the world was basically fully-dilated, 90% effaced. I remember hanging out and smoking weed with Jon Duchin, an old friend who never left Miami for college. Jon always loved music. Loud music. *Good* loud music. Whenever. Wherever. In his car, in his parents' house, and in each of the hellhole apartments he lived in between 1989 and 1993. There was nobody whose musical taste I respected more than Jon's.

That first summer, Jon Duchin got grunged. Led Zeppelin and the Who mutated into a steady stream of Soundgarden, Alice in Chains, Stone Temple Pilots, Pearl Jam. And yes, of course: Nirvana. Jon had totally bought in.

I did not. Why?

I just didn't hear it. It meant nothing to me. I *wanted* to want it. But I didn't.

Now, this isn't to say I didn't *appreciate* grunge, at least in one critical regard: it immediately nuked the big-hair-makeup-crotch-less-cheesy-ass-EVH-rip-off-LA-glam-shitmetal bands. Instantly. So, for that, I was grateful.

But on a gut level, why was I untouched?

Maybe it was the hackysack-circle vibe I had just settled into. For all of grunge's power, there's a negativity to it that just hit me at the wrong angle, at the wrong time. Kurt Cobain and Nirvana, the High Priests of Grunge, aren't merely rebellious: they are nihilistic, cutting, angry. No laughing. No fun. This was "serious."

Now, "serious" I can handle. But on another level - musicianship - I gotta say, to my ears no new ground was being broken. Melody? Nope. Harmony? Go fuck yourself. Smells Like Teen Spirit? I like the Weird Al Yankovic version better. Depressed, drugged out, scummy, sweaty looking young adults growling pretentious and juvenile lyrics about how much their lives suck ass? Sorry gents, I'm out.

Bottom line: Cobain's stuff reminded me of the songs I wrote in high school. And, believe me, that's not a compliment to myself.

And I never grew into it, either. The only compromise I made was when grunge started to bend towards *me:* like when Eddie Vedder and Pearl Jam started making sweet, soulful, acoustic stuff. *That* I could get with. And I love it to this day.

But since the too-short life of Kurt Cobain never allowed for a second, mellower phase - Nirvana remained, and remains, that thing for my friends, not myself. Even in my soul-baring musical conversations, Nirvana is still the subject I'm trying to change.

I'll stick with my Beatles, and, yes, my Dylan.

ABOUT THE AUTHORS

Joshua Shelov *Bob Dylan* **(+ book editor)** Joshua has co-written two feature films (*Green Street Hooligans,* starring Elijah Wood, and *The Best and the Brightest,* starring Neil Patrick Harris), and co-directed two ESPN *30 for 30* documentaries (*#bringbacksungwoo,* *WE ARE*). He created and taught the seminar *Storytelling for the Screen* at Yale University. Joshua lives in Connecticut with his wife and three beautiful, Dylan-deprived children. Blog: http://www.joshuashelov.com.

Amy Wilson *Tom Waits* Amy is the author of *When Did I Get Like This?* (HarperCollins) and has written for magazines like *Redbook* and websites like *The New York Times.* She is the co-host of a new podcast called *What Fresh Hell: Laughing in the Face of Motherhood.* She is also an actor - check out http://www.amywilson.com.

Alex Funk *Eric Clapton* Alex Funk is a researcher and educator based in Baltimore. He has degrees in music, literature, and linguistics, and plays most games.

Danielle Delgado *Carole King* Danielle is an actress living in New York City. She reveres David Bowie, old dogs, and key lime pie, and will help you see the errors of your ways if you don't.

Aimee Weingart Pollak *The Who* Aimee is a public interest lawyer, half-assed wife and mother, and genuinely bad cook. Her musical talents are limited to performing drunken karaoke and harassing her son to practice guitar. What she lacks in knowledge of musical theory or performance ability, she more than makes up for in strongly held opinions and biases. The first record she ever purchased was Barry Manilow's Greatest Hits and she still knows all the words to Mandy and Copacabana.

Jason Barker *U2* Jason Barker is an infectious diseases physician and researcher. He briefly played guitar in band for a living and can only dream of having been as good at it as U2.

Brian Alverson *The Beatles* Brian Alverson is a pediatric hospitalist physician, researcher and professor at Brown University. He plays violin and fiddle, and no, dammit, those aren't the same thing.

Dave Bauer *Billy Joel* Dave Bauer lives with his three cats in the Dakota Badlands. Dave Bauer is 5'4", bald and muscular. Dave Bauer never travels anywhere without his mandolin, shark-tooth necklace and red leather jacket. Dave Bauer is lying about all of the above so Billy Joel won't be able to track him down and punch him in the face.

James Michels *John Coltrane* James is a systems project leader at Jacobi Medical Center's Information Technology Department. He lives in Scarsdale, NY with family including two Siberian Forest cats with whom he has a mutual respect.

Andrew McLaughlin *The Smiths* Andrew is an influencer, having won second place in Fargo, North Dakota's prestigious Northern Lights Council of Cub Scouts Annual Balsa Wood Racer competition in 1980.

Cebra Graves *The Rolling Stones* Cebra is an education strategist and a father, rarely simultaneously. He lives along the 8th mile of the NYC Marathon route, which is easily the best one of the 26. In a former life, he was Pierre Menard's ghostwriter. Nowadays, he listens to whatever his kids want to listen to, but that doesn't mean he has to enjoy it.

Nancy Anderson *Frank Sinatra* Nancy is a Brooklyn-based Olivier-award nominated actress and singer devoted to the American Songbook. She is the winner of The Noel Coward Cabaret Competition Award, and her CD of 20s and 30s jazz is available at www.nancyanderson.name

Ryan McGee *James Taylor* is a senior writer at ESPN, primarily working the redneck beat of motorsports and college football.

The worst-selling author of two books lives in Charlotte, NC with his wife, daughter and dog.

Seth Morgulas *Igor Stravinsky* Seth is an officer in the United States Army, currently serving as a battalion commander in the Middle East.

Alicia Biggart *Pearl Jam* Alicia is a film and television producer who has worked for Vice Media, P3 Entertainment, and J. Walter Thompson.

Michelle Brazier *Richard Wagner* Michelle Brazier is a freelance violinist by night and an English professor by day. She has played back-up for Ray Charles, kd lang, and Plácido Domingo. But mostly, these days, she teaches reading and writing sentences and paragraphs, and spends time with her two kids and wife in New Jersey.

Alex Buono *Bob Marley* Alex is an Oscar-nominated filmmaker whose credits include director/executive producer of the Emmy-nominated comedy series *Documentary Now!*, along with writer/producer of the feature documentary *Bigger Stronger Faster** and producer/cinematographer of *Green Street Hooligans*. Alex lives in Los Angeles with his wife, filmmaker Tamsin Rawady, and their two daughters.

Jaclyn Reindorf Savolainen *Led Zeppelin* Jaclyn is an academic librarian living in Rhinebeck, NY, with her husband, two children and too many pets. True to the librarian stereotype, Jaclyn loves knitting, cats and tea, and strongly dislikes loud noises.

Leslie DiNicola *Al Green* Nationally-acclaimed singer-songwriter Leslie DiNicola has a rare gift for the sonic snapshot. Through the poetic accessibility of her writing style, she captures personal moments with a universal perspective. As a live performer, her commanding vocals and smoldering stage presence have enabled her to frequently tour worldwide alongside renowned artists such as Brian Wilson, John Waite, American Idol winner Lee Dewyze, and many more.

Christine M. Caddick *Bruce Springsteen* Christine is a former producer at ESPN specializing in long-form features and documentaries. She is the winner of eight Emmy Awards and is currently producing the lives of a sixteen-year-old daughter and fourteen-year-old son.

Marc Chalpin *Barbra Streisand* When not hating on Barbra Streisand, Marc Chalpin is a tax attorney by training and currently works as the CFO in his family's business. Marc comes from a family of talented singers and dancers, and even one producer who worked with Jimi Hendrix, but his only musical talent is entertaining a few drunk people on occasion in karaoke, and maybe play a kazoo.

Steve J. Rogers *John Lennon* Steve is a freelance content contributor to sites such as PlaceToBeNation.com, TheBatmanUniverse.net, and NYSportsDay.com., as well as a social media coordinator for a couple of New Jersey based film fests, Brightside Tavern Film Festival in Jersey City and Hang onto Your Shorts Film Festival in Asbury Park.

Julian Sheppard *Counting Crows* Julian is the co-writer of the film *Complete Unknown,* and a Drama Desk-Nominated Playwright. People still talk about his Air Band performance of The Who's "You Better You Bet" at his Jewish sleepaway camp. So take that, Adam Duritz's dreadlocks!

Patti Weiser *Paul McCartney* Patti has been a lawyer and a movie producer. She is currently enjoying the best job ever: Mom. She would like to credit Robert Weiser with being supportive and a great partner in each of these careers. She also saw Paul McCartney in concert this past summer and thought it was an amazing show. Go figure.

Jacqui Robbins *James Taylor, vol. 2* Jacqui is the author of the books *The New Girl...And Me* and *Two of a Kind* (both illustrated by Matt Phelan and published by Atheneum/Simon & Schuster). She currently works as a preschool teacher for children with special needs, where her songwriting credits include "The Ramadan Song," "I'm a Little Caterpillar," and the second verse of "Autumn Leaves Are Falling Down." All of which qualifies her to make sweeping criticism of one of the world's most beloved artists. Obviously.

Mark Badger *Leonard Cohen* Mark is creative director for a digital agency based in Richmond, Virginia, leading teams in the design of apps and websites for brands you love, but also other brands. Raised on a healthy diet of 70s soft rock, the serendipitous gift of a Time Life cassette tape led him inexorably toward a lifelong appreciation of Prince, Bowie, and Stevie Wonder. To this day, he is grateful for *AM Gold '77*.

Jeff Brock *Wolfgang Amadeus Mozart* Jeffrey is chair of the mathematics department at Brown University.

Greg Raskin *Steely Dan* Greg Raskin works at Memorial Sloan Kettering Cancer Center. He was briefly in a rock band in high school, and his band-mates agreed that his sole positive contribution was coming up with the name, The Harmonic Convergence -- which Greg believes holds up even today.

Henry Tenney *Stevie Wonder* Henry is a writer/producer from the real home of punk rock (Cleveland) who nitpicks the greats because he cares.

Ron Wechsler *Tom Waits, vol. 2* Ron Wechsler has been a media executive for over 20 years, beginning his career in independent film working on the seminal films Kids, Beautiful Girls, and Scream and then co-producing The House Of Yes. He then shifted to sports television, where he spent nearly a decade with ESPN helping to oversee projects as varied as *The Contender* and *Mayne Street.* Most recently, Wechsler has served as a Senior Vice President for NBC Sports, where he runs the Original Programming unit. Wechsler lives in Mamaroneck, NY with his wife Laura and two children Trent and Ben. He is also a guy that spends a lot of time taking pictures of food and craft beer.

Neil Turitz *The Grateful Dead* Neil is a journalist and filmmaker who has been working in and writing about Hollywood for close to two decades. He is the main columnist for the entertainment news magazine *The Tracking Board,* where his column appears three times each week. You can tweet him at @neilturitz. Do so, and he will more than likely respond.

Elizabeth Jayne Liu *Macklemore* lives in Austin with her family and her complete collection of Yo! MTV Raps Trading Cards. She writes about the many incarnations of her life, from trap queen to PTA mom, and her affinity for all things hip hop at www.flourishinprogress.com

Michael Fass *Nirvana* Michael is a lawyer. He lives in Fairfield, CT, with his beautiful wife, Sarah, his three sons, Ethan, Owen and Zeke, and his beloved dog, Stanny. He also sweats profusely when he plays guitar.

For more information on the THERE, I SAID IT series, visit:

http://www.joshuashelov.com